増刊 CreAtor 13

Espoir
エスポワール

Bead Loom Collection

煌めくビーズ織りの世界

豊田里子作品集
Satoko Toyoda

目 次

藤壺「源氏物語」　3
Fujitsubo The Tale of Genji

フリンジネックレス　4
Fringe Necklace

ゆれる桜　5
Fluttering Cherry Blossom Necklace

バイオレットネックレス　6
Violet Necklace

カメリヤ　7
Camellia

ダイヤモンドパターンネックレス　8
Diamond Pattern Necklace

小花のオールドローズ 幅広ラリエット　9
Wide Lariat: Small Old Roses

幸せを呼ぶハミング・バード　10
A Hummingbird Bringing Happiness

海の彼方をながめるバタフライ　11
A Butterfly Looking beyond the Sea

赤くかがやく アムレットパース　12
Shining Red Amulet Purse

ジャポニズム　13
Japonism

品のあるスミレのロングラリエット　14
Elegant Pansy Lariat

舞うゴージャスな蝶　15
Dancing Gorgeous Butterfly Necklace

オールドローズに恋して　16
Fall in Love with Old Roses

細くゆれるバイオレットブレスレット　17
Slander and Swingy Violet Bracelet

私のお気に入りの薔薇　18
My Favorite Roses

待 宵　19
Waiting for the Evening

藤壺ネックレス・イヤリング　20
Fujitsubo Necklace and Earrings

透けて煌めく陽気な花達　21
Happy Transparent Sparkling Flowers

煌めく玉手箱　22
Sparkling Treasure Chest

エスポワール　23
Espoir

煌 煌　24
Brilliant

翔　25
Fly-High

萌黄色の中に舞う桜　26
The Elegant Bead Partition with Fluttering Cherry Blossoms

里山の夕焼け　28
The Sunset in Rural Area

ハッピーロード　30
Happy Road

ウエディングベア　32
Wedding Bear

クリスマスまであと何日？　33
How many days until Christmas?

メリークリスマス（サンタ村から）　34
Merry Christmas from the Santa Clous Village

ビーズ織りの作り方　36
HOW TO MAKE

藤 壺 「源氏物語」
Fujitsubo The Tale of Genji
W49×D34×H44cm

フリンジネックレス
Fringe Necklace

ゆれる桜
Fluttering Cherry Blossom Necklace

バイオレットネックレス
Violet Necklace

カメリヤ
Camellia

ダイヤモンドパターンネックレス
Diamond Pattern Necklace

小花のオールドローズ 幅広ラリエット
Wide Lariat: Small Old Roses

幸せを呼ぶハミング・バード
A Hummingbird Bringing Happiness

海の彼方をながめるバタフライ
A Butterfly Looking beyond the Sea

赤くかがやくアムレットパース
Shining Red Amulet Purse

ジャポニズム
Japonism

品のあるスミレのロングラリエット
Elegant Pansy Lariat

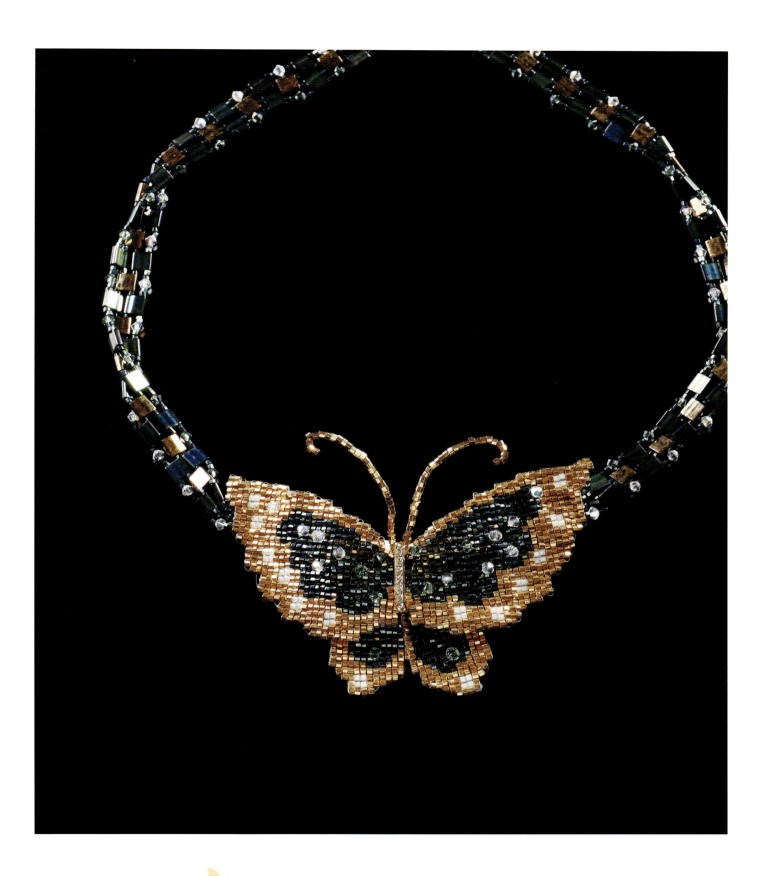

舞うゴージャスな蝶
Dancing Gorgeous Butterfly Necklace

HOW TO MAKE_p.36

オールドローズに恋して
Fall in Love with Old Roses

細くゆれるバイオレットブレスレット
Slender and Swingy Violet Bracelet

私のお気に入りの薔薇
My Favorite Roses

 待宵
Waiting for the Evening

藤壺ネックレス・イヤリング
Fujitsubo Necklace and Earrings

透けて煌めく陽気な花達
Happy Transparent Sparkling Flowers

煌めく玉手箱
Sparkling Treasure Chest

エスポワール
Espoir

W41×D41×H50cm

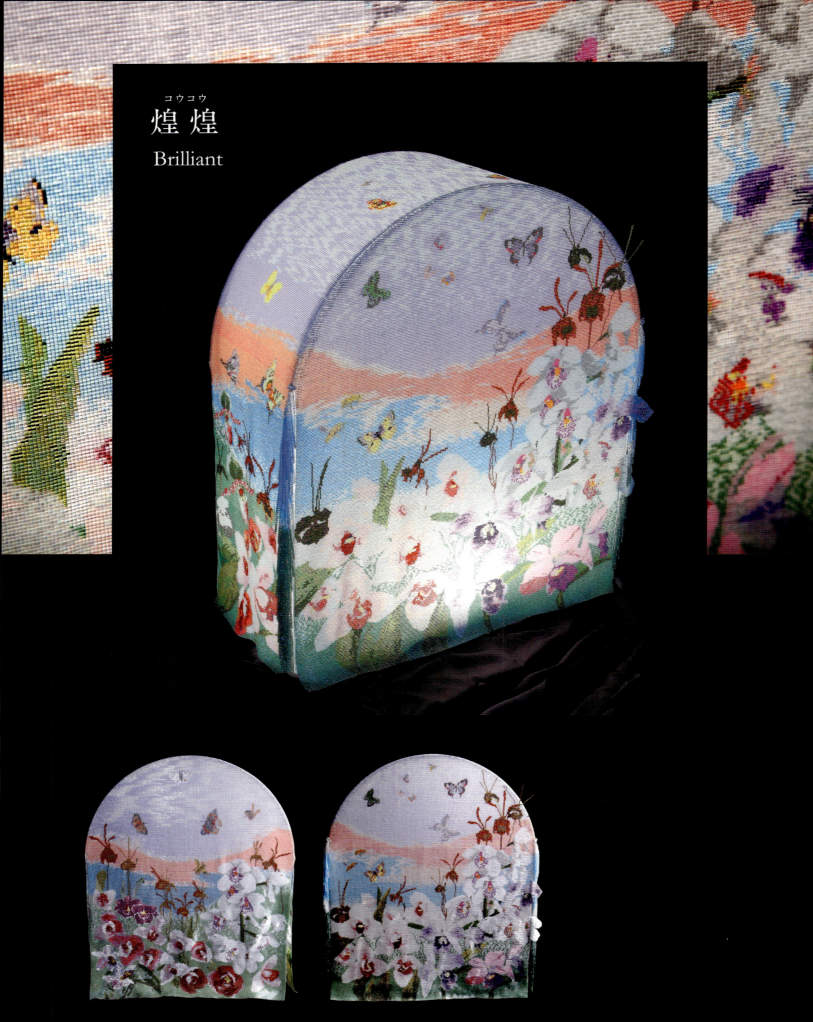

煌 煌
コウコウ
Brilliant

翔
Fly-High

萌黄色の中に舞う桜
The Elegant Bead Partition
　with Fluttering Cherry Blossoms

タペストリー：W140×H180cm

里山の夕焼け
The Sunset in Rural Area

ハッピーロード
Happy Road
HOW TO MAKE_p.41

クリスマスまであと何日？
How many days until Christmas?

メリークリスマス（サンタ村から）
Merry Christmas from Santa Clous Village

舞うゴージャスな蝶 ネックレス －作品 p.15 －
Dancing Gorgeous Butterfly Necklace

材料
- A DB-23cut　99コ
- B DB-27cut　716コ
- C DB-31cut　476コ
- D DB-52　　　56コ
- TL457　28コ
- TL468　58コ
- スワロフスキー SW 5301/3　#17　50コ
- スワロフスキー SW 5328/3　#357　49コ

他の材料（MIYUKI）
- ロンデル　K1471G
- クラスプ　F#49
- ワイヤー　#30
- ビーズ織り専用テグス
- 針　　　　DF-834

Materials
- Delica Size 11° (MIYUKI)
- 99 pcs DB-23 (Hex Cut)
- 716 pcs DB-27 (Hex Cut)
- 476 pcs DB-31 (Hex Cut)
- 56 pcs DB-52
- 28 pcs Tila Beads H5993 TL457
- 58 pcs Tila Beads H5995 TL468
- 50 pcs SW crystal 5301/3 #17
- 49 pcs SW crystal 5328/3 #357

Other Materials: MIYUKI
- 3 pcs SW Rondelle K1471 G
- Clasp F #49
- Craft Wire G-30, Brass
- Illusion Cord (Monofilament) DF839 #40
- Needle DF-834

蝶のパーツ A / Gorgeous Butterfly Necklace A

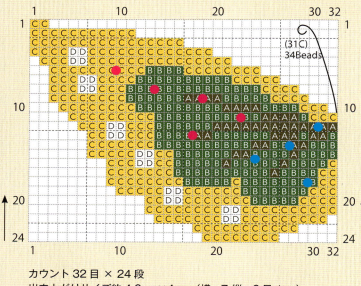

カウント 32目×24段
出来上がりサイズ約 4.6cm×4cm（横：7 縦：6目/cm）
Columns and Rows (32 columns × 24 rows)
Size of the sheet when completed 4.57cm × 4cm

蝶のパーツ B / Gorgeous Butterfly Necklace B

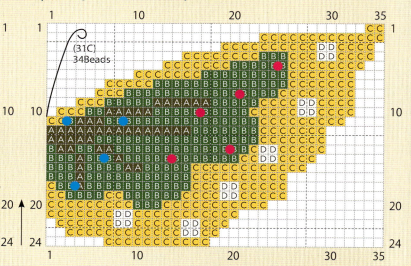

カウント 35目×24段
出来上がりサイズ約 5cm×4cm（横：7 縦：6目/cm）
Columns and Rows (35 columns × 24 rows)
Size of the sheet when completed 5cm × 4cm

蝶のパーツ C　2枚 / Gorgeous Butterfly Necklace C

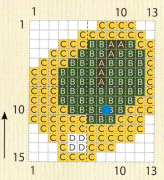

カウント 13目×15段
出来上がりサイズ 約1.9cm×2.5cm
（横：7 縦：6目/cm）
Columns and Rows
(13 columns × 15 rows)
Size of the sheet when
completed 1.85cm × 2.5cm

A. カラーテーブル（Delica） / A. Colors and Symbols of Beads (Delica)
A	23C	(42コ)
B	27C	(164コ)
C	31C	(272コ)
D	52	(24コ)
●	SW 5301/3 #17	(5コ)
●	SW 5328/3 #357	(4コ)

B. カラーテーブル（Delica） / B. Colors and Symbols of Beads (Delica)
A	23C	(45コ)
B	27C	(198コ)
C	31C	(278コ)
D	52	(24コ)
●	SW 5301/3 #17	(5コ)
●	SW 5328/3 #357	(4コ)

C. カラーテーブル（Delica） / C. Colors and Symbols of Beads (Delica)
A	23C	(12コ)
B	27C	(116コ)
C	31C	(166コ)
D	52	(8コ)
●	SW 5328/3 #357	(2コ)

2枚分

羽の組み立て方（1枚ずつ織った羽を合わせる）
How to Assemble the Individually Loomed Wings

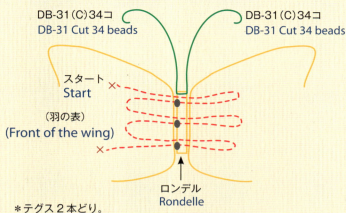
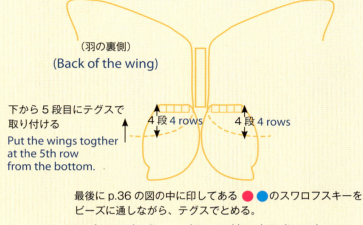

* テグス2本どり。
* スタートでヨコ糸にテグスを結びつけ、ビーズに通す。
* ロンデルの穴をくぐらせ、反対側の羽に通す。
* 戻って、また同じロンデルの穴を通る。
* 順番に通して羽を完成させる。

* Double-stranded thread.
* Make a knot at the start of beading and thread the beads.
* Thread through the hole of rondelle, then thread the same hole of the rondelle.
* Come back to the other wing and thread through the same hole of the rondelle.

触角の付け方
How to Attach the Antenna

ワイヤー10cmをロンデルの穴に通し、左右DB-31（C）を34粒ずつ通して先端を丸めてワイヤーを処理する。

Thread a 10 cm (3.9 in) wire into the hole of the rondelle, and thread 34 DB-31 Cut beads each on the left and right sides, then finish the wire by rounding the edge.

チェーンの付け方
How to Attach the Chains

テグス2本どり 2.5m用意
Prepare 2.5 meters (98.4 inches) of double-stranded thread.

6段目1目奥から付ける（反対側も同じ）
Attach from the end of the first column to the 6th row. (Same for the opposite side.)

- 14列　14個（TL457）×2＝28コ
  28 pcs, 2 x 14 pcs/14 rows (TL457)
- 15列　29個（TL468）×2＝58コ
  58 pcs, 2 x 29 pcs/15 rows (TL468)
- SW 5301/3 #17　40コ
  40 pcs SW crystal 5301/3 #17
- SW 5328/3 #357　39コ
  39 pcs SW crystal 5328/3 #357

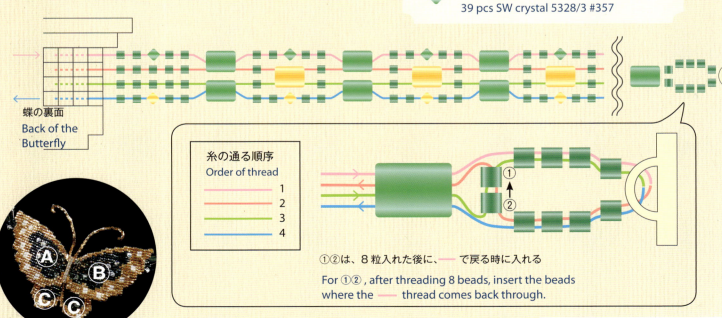

①②は、8粒入れた後に、— で戻る時に入れる
For ①②, after threading 8 beads, insert the beads where the — thread comes back through.

蝶のネックレス
How to make Dancing Gorgeous Butterfly Necklace

ウエディングベア – 作品 p.32 – (織り図→p.41)
Wedding Bear

材料（ウエディングベア2体の分量）	Materials (for 2 wedding bears)
デリカビーズ（MIYUKI）	Delica Size 11° (MIYUKI)
DB-202　20g　5箱	5 x 20g DB-202
DB-1534　20g　5箱	5 x 20g DB-1534
ビーズステッチ糸 K4570 #2　3コ	3 bobbins Beading Thread K4570 #2
ビーズステッチ糸 K4570 #14　3コ	3 bobbins Beading Thread K4570 #14
他の材料	Other Materials:
目　7mm グラスアイ　2コずつ	Eyes: 2 pcs 7mm Glass eyes
4つ穴ボタン(直径1cm位)　4コずつ	4 pcs 1cm across 4-Hole button
化繊綿　適量	Chemical fiber batting

ベアの組み立て方

① 各部分のダーツをとじる（頭・胴体・耳）★印

1. Close darts of the head, body and ears.

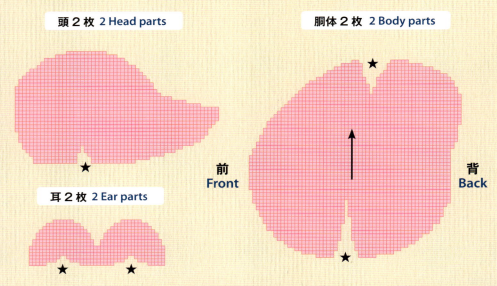

頭2枚 2 Head parts　　胴体2枚 2 Body parts　　耳2枚 2 Ear parts　　前 Front　　背 Back

〔とじ方　How to close〕
※ →　矢印に添って、ビーズステッチ糸をビーズの中に通し、とじる
* Thread onto the beads as indicated by the arrow to close darts.

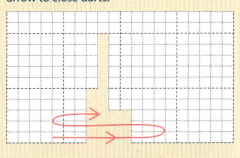

② → で示した通り、各部分をとじ合わせていく。綿を入れる為に上部はあけておく。

2. As indicated by the arrow, stitch the beads together. Leave the top part open for stuffing.

手4枚(2枚ずつ) 4 Arm parts (2 each)　　胴体2枚 2 Body parts　　耳2枚(たたんだ図) 2 Ear parts (folded)

※糸はビーズの中をくぐること
*Beading thread should thread through the beads

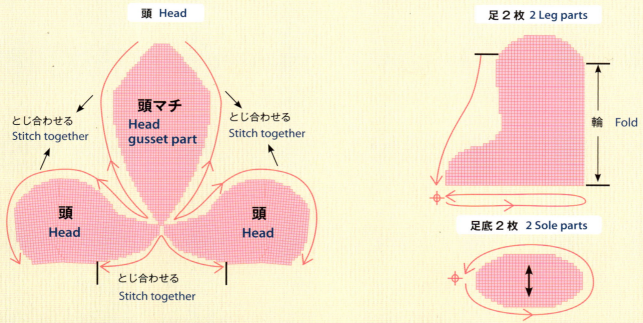

③ 頭・胴体・手・足をとじ合わせたら、それぞれに綿を詰める。(しっかり固く綿を入れるのがコツ)
3. Stitch together the head, body, arms and legs, respectively, then stuff each part with batting. (Make sure to stuff firmly.)

④ 綿を詰め終わったら、その部分をとじる。
4. After stuffing, close the open part.

⑤ 耳と首をとじ合わせる。(縫い糸2本どり)
5. Stitch the ears and neck. (Use 2 strands of thread.)

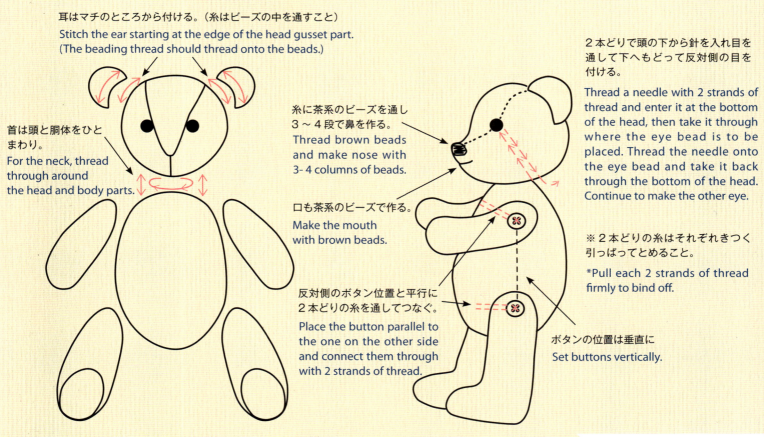

How to make Wedding Bear

ウエディングベアの織り図
Wedding Bear

頭 2 枚 2 Head parts

胴体 2 枚 2 Body parts

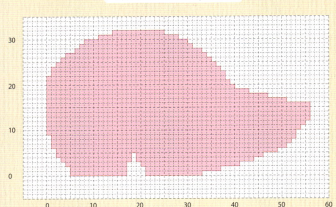

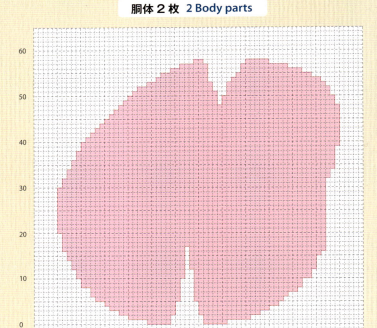

手 4 枚 4 Arm parts

耳 2 枚 2 Ear parts

頭マチ 1 枚 1 Head gusset part

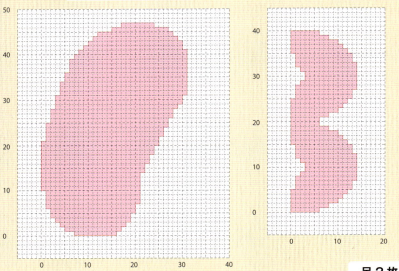

足 2 枚 2 Leg parts

足底 2 枚 2 Foot base parts

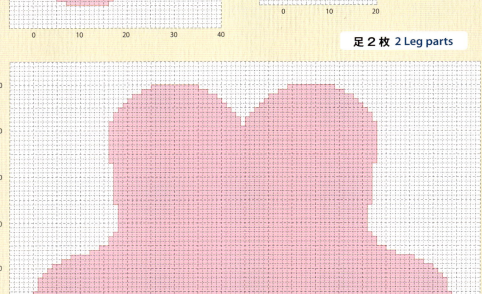

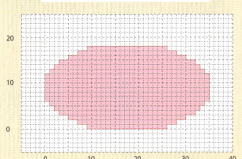

ウエディングベア
Wedding Bear

ブブロン村 木組みの家 – 作品 p.30 –
Village Of Beuvron En Auge

材料 Materials

Delica Size 11° (MIYUKI)

A	DB-732 × 2553	G	DB-351 × 326	N	DB-682 × 156	W	DB-271 × 172
B	DB-6 × 2379	H	DB-110 × 104	O	DB-43 × 234	X	DB-651 × 22
C	DB-84 × 148	J	DB-656 × 364	P	DB-683 × 232	Y	DB-764 × 6
D	DB-1584 × 2216	K	DB-724 × 84	S	DB-653 × 70	Z	DB-709 × 86
E	DB-10 × 111	L	DB-852 × 123	T	DB-749 × 132	@	DB-853 × 44
F	DB-794 × 535	M	DB-602 × 219	V	DB-150 × 32		

ビーズステッチ糸 K4570 #3 3コ   3 bobbins Beading Thread K4570 #3

① 目数表に沿って、4枚のシートを織る。
1. Weave 4 beaded parts according to the beading patterns.

② 4面のシートを縫い合わせて、箱型に仕上げる。
2. Sew the 4 parts together into a box shape.

③ ボール紙を使って、織りシートより少し小さな箱型を作り、織ったシートをかぶせて完成。
3. Make a cardboard box slightly smaller and put it in the house.

正面 Front

側面2枚・後面 Back, Side

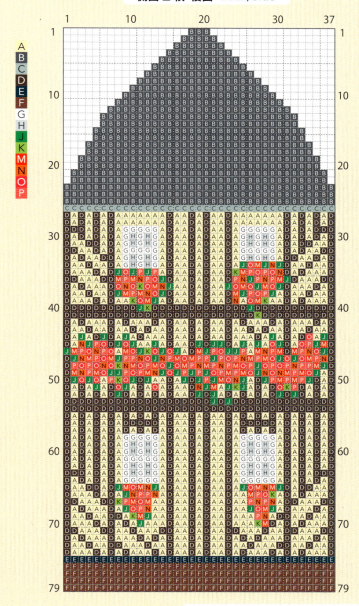

ブブロン村 木組みの家
Village Of Beuvron En Auge

人形とドレス －作品 p.30－
Doll & Dress

型紙使用時は140％拡大コピー

材料（出来上がり10cm）

綿ジャージ肌色（顔・ボディ・手）
　20cm × 14cm
洗濯ネット（ボディ）
　のりがついていない、使用したものが良い
丸小ビーズ　黒2個（目）
25番刺しゅう糸
　黒（目）、こげ茶（まゆ毛）、ピンク（口）
ボール紙　4cm × 4cm（ボディ底）
フェルト　4cm × 4cm（ボディ底）
刺子用糸　茶一束（髪の毛）
化繊綿　適量
キルト糸　生成

道具

縫い針、まち針、はさみ、定規、竹串、
ミシン、目打ち、木工用接着剤、ほお紅

Materials (Finished size 10cm tall)

20cm x 14cm Fresh colored cotton jersey cloth (Face, Body and Arm)
Laundry net: Not starched. Used one is sufficed. (Body)
2 pcs Size 11° seed beads: Black (Eye)
Embroidery thread (#25): Black (Eye), Dark brown (Eyebrow) and Pink (Mouth)
4cm × 4cm Cardboard (Base)
4cm × 4cm Felt (Base)
Sashiko (Japanese embroidery) thread: Brown (Hair)
Chemical fiber batting
Quilting thread: Unbleached or Cream

Tools

Needle, Marking pins, Scissors, Ruler, Bamboo skewer, Sewing machine, Eyeleteer, Glue & Cheek rouge

1 頭を作る　1. Make the head.

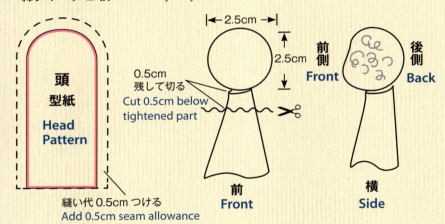

綿ジャージ2枚　2 Cotton jersey cloths
0.5cm残して切る　Cut 0.5cm below tightened part
頭型紙　Head Pattern
縫い代 0.5cm つける　Add 0.5cm seam allowance
前側 Front　後側 Back
前 Front　横 Side

①ミシン、または手縫い（細かく）でまわりを縫う。
1. Sew around the head on a sewing machine or hand-stitch.

②ほおが出るように丸く形を作りながら、綿を押し込むように固く詰めていく。（菜箸などの先の丸いもの使用）
2. Stuff the head with batting and shape the cheek parts to slightly stand out. The head should be firmly stuffed. Use a chopstick or a stick that has a blunt end for stuffing.

③キルト糸2本どりで首の部分の後ろをひと針すくって2～3回ぐるぐる巻いて絞り、後ろで縫い止める。縫い止めた下から0.5cm残して切る。
3. Thread a needle with 2 strands of quilting thread and take a small stitch at the back of the neck and wind around 2-3 times, then tighten and sew together. Leave 0.5cm of cloth at the bottom and cut out the rest.

2 ボディ、手を作る　2. Make the body and arms.

①綿ジャージを中表にして、その上下にネットを重ねる。（綿ジャージだけでは綿の入れ具合で伸びてしまうので、伸び止めに使用）
1. Place the cotton jersey cloths on top of each other, right sides together and then layer one laundry net on the top and another one on the bottom. (Laundry net is used to prevent the cloth from stretching when the batting is stuffed.)

綿ジャージ2枚・ネット2枚
Layer 2 cotton jersey cloths and 2 laundry nets as below.

ネット　Laundry net
綿ジャージ　Cotton jersey cloth
綿ジャージ　Cotton jersey cloth
ネット　Laundry net

切り込み　Make a cut
あき口　Turning gap
ボディ型紙　Body Pattern
縫い代 0.5cm つける　Add 0.5cm seam allowance

綿ジャージ2枚　2 Cotton jersey cloths
手型紙　Arm Pattern
縫い代 0.5cm つける　Add 0.5cm seam allowance

②あき口から下までミシン縫いして表に返す。（手縫いの場合は2本どりで細かく）
2. Sew around the body on a sewing machine, leaving a turning gap at the top. When hand stitching, use 2 strands of thread and sew together very finely. Turn the body right side out through the turning gap.

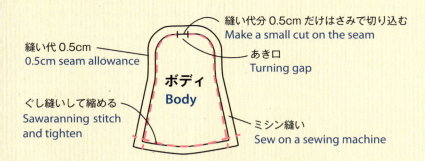

③ボディは高さ6.5cm位になるように綿を詰めて、出来上がり線をぐし縫いで縮めてとめる。縫い代はでこぼこしない程度に中に押し込むように入れる。

3. Stuff the body with batting and make it approximately 6.5cm tall. Sew a running stitch at the bottom finishing line and tighten. Put the seam inside evenly.

④フエルト、ボール紙を2枚貼り合わせてボディの縫い縮めた面に貼る。

4. Paste the felt and cardboard together and attach it to the bottom of the body.

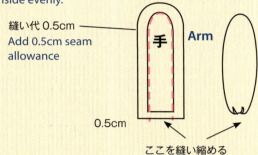

⑤手も同様に縫って目打ちを使用して表に返す。綿を詰めて出来上がり線を縫い縮めて絞り、縫い代を中に入れる。

5. Same as what you did to make the body, sew around the arm and turn right side out using a stiletto. Stuff the arm with batting, sew on the bottom finishing line, then tighten and put the seam inside.

※手は型紙が小さいので縫った後に縫い代を0.1〜0.2mm切り落とす。切りすぎないように。

* Once you have sewn the arm, cut it out approximately 0.1-0.2mm outside the sewn line. Be aware not to cut it out too much.

③ 頭とボディ・手をつける | 3. Attach the head and arms to the body.

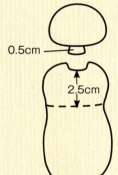

①ボディのあき口を菜箸などで少し押し、くぼみをつける。頭の下の縫い縮めた部分を入れてまち針で2、3カ所止めて、コの字で縫い合わせる。

1. Push the turning gap of the body with a chopstick or something similar to make a well. Put the bottom part of the head into the well and sew together so the seam line resembles a U-shape.

(点は布地の中)
(Dotted line indicates the thread under the cloth.)

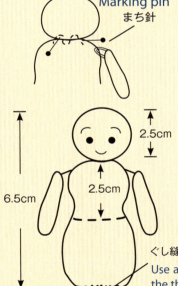

②手はボディの肩先にボタン付けのように2本どりで2回くらい渡して2〜3回巻きつけてボディに止める。

2. Use 2 strands of thread and sew the arm into the shoulder part of the body twice, similar to stitching a button on a shirt.

③ボディの2.5cm下を糸1本でぐし縫いして（綿をすくって縫ってもOK）縮めてウエストラインを作る。

3. Sew a running stitch with a single strand of thread at 2.5 cm below the top of the body and tighten it to make it look like the body has a waist. When using a running stitch, it is ok to thread into the batting.

ぐし縫いして糸を引き締める。
Use a running stitch and then tighten the thread.

④ 顔を作る | 4. Make the face.

ストレートステッチ（こげ茶）
Straight stitch (Dark Brown)

黒刺しゅう糸2本どり
Black embroidery threads
(Use 2 strand of thread)

ほお紅
Cheek rough

ストレートステッチ（ピンク）
Straight stitch (Pink)

黒ビーズを1個通してから横に針を入れて頭部に出す。同じことをもう1回繰り返しビーズに2回糸を通す。

Thread a black bead onto the needle first and thread it onto the head. Repeat it again and thread the embroidery thread twice into the bead.

①目の位置はまち針や消えるチャコペンなど使用して決める。刺しゅう糸はすべて2本どりで、頭から針を刺して、まゆ毛、口はストレートステッチで刺して表情を作り、また頭部へ出して玉止めする。

1. Decide where you want to have the eyes and mark them on the face with marking pins or tailor's chalk. Thread the needle with 2 strand of embroidery thread and enter the needle at the top of the head, then sew a straight stitch for eyebrows and mouth. Thread the needle back to the top of the head and finish with a knot.

人形とドレス
How to make Doll & Dress

⑤ 髪の毛をつける　5. Attach Hair.

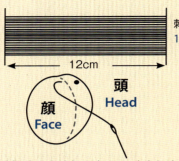
刺子用糸 100本
100 Strands of thread
顔 Face
頭 Head

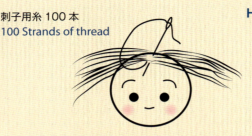

頭側 Head side
接着剤 Glue
顔側 Face side

① 刺子糸のよりをほどいて1本をとり出し、2本どりで頭から針を入れてひたいに出す。

Thread a needle with 2 strands of Sashiko (Japanese embroidery) thread, and thread it onto the head and take it through the forehead.

② すくった位置に髪の中央をのせて、糸を渡して綿ごとすくって、ひたい側に出して糸を引く。糸を渡した中央に針を入れ、また頭側に出して玉止めする。

Place the hair on the thread, and thread the needle again onto the head and take it through the forehead. Enter the needle right at the top of the head (center of the hair), then take it through the head and finish with a knot.

③ 髪を上にあげて竹串に接着剤をつけて頭全体に塗る。髪を下げてクシでとかして整えて接着する。顔の横も同様にして接着する。長さは好みでカットする。

Pull the hair up and apply glue using a stick as thin as a bamboo skewer. Put the hair down, comb and stick onto the head. Do it the same way for the hair on the face side. Cut the hair, if desired.

※三つ編みは6本を2本ずつで編み込む。好みの位置にのせて止める。（糸の長さは12〜14cmで編む）

*When making braids, use 2 batches of 6 embroidery threads and weave into braids. Place the braids as desired and tie up. (Prepare 12-14cm threads to make braids)

ドレスの仕上げ方　How to Finish the Dress

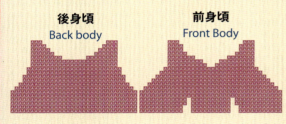
後身頃 Back body
前身頃 Front Body

① 前身頃のダーツを縫う（ビーズの中を通して、縫い合わせる）
1. Sew darts on the front body. (Thread the beading thread through the beads)

② 片方の脇、肩を縫う（ビーズの中を通して、縫い合わせる）
2. Sew together one side of the body and shoulder respectively. (Thread the beading thread through the beads.)

③ もう片方は、人形に着せてから縫い合わせる。
3. Put the dress on the doll and sew together the other side of the body and shoulder.

材料　Materials

デリカビーズ（MIYUKI）　Delica Size 15° (MIYUKI)
A　DBS-295　5g×2箱（3014コ）　3014 pcs 2×5g DBS-295
ビーズステッチ糸 K4570 #8　2コ　2×Beading Thread K4570 #8

ドレス前後身頃　Front and Back body

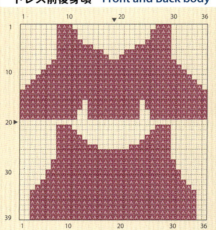

カウント 36目×39段
出来上がりサイズ約 4.5cm×5.6cm
（横：8 縦：7目／cm）
Columns and Rows (36 Columns × 39 rows)
Size of the sheet when completed 4.5cm×5.6cm

カラーテーブル（Delica）
Colors and Symbols of Beads (Delica Size 15°)
A　■　DBS295　（908コ）

ドレススカート　Skirt

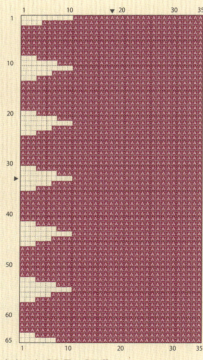

カウント 35目×65段
出来上がりサイズ約 4.4cm×9.3cm
（横：8 縦：7目／cm）
Columns and Rows (35 Columns × 65 rows)
Size of the sheet when completed 4.4cm×9.3cm

カラーテーブル（Delica）
Colors and Symbols of Beads (Delica Size 15°)
A　■　DBS295　（2,106コ）

④ スカートの糸引きをする。
4. Pull the working thread of the skirt.

⑤ →から糸を引きはじめると、右側にダーツを寄せる時にスムーズに仕上げることが出来る。
5. Start pulling the thread from the left. It makes it easier to close the darts on the right side.

⑥ スカートの糸引きが終わったら、身頃にとじ合わせる。
6. When finished with pulling the thread on the skirt, sew it onto the upper-body of the dress.

⑦ スカートの脇、片方の脇、片方の肩は、人形に着せてから縫い合わせる。
7. Put the skirt on the doll and sew the sides together.

ビーズ織りの基礎
Basic Beading on a Loom

ビーズ織りは、専用の織り機を使いヨコ糸に通したビーズを織って作り出します。
小さなアイテムから、織ったものを組み合わせることで大きな作品や立体をつくることもできます。
一般のビーズで制作することもできますが、織用に開発された円筒形ビーズ（デリカビーズ）を使うと、ビーズ同士の隙間ができないので、より表面が滑らかに仕上がり図案も鮮明に表現することができます。
織用のビーズは1000色を超える豊富な色数と種類があり、それらを組み合わせることで表現は無限なものとなります。

ビーズ織りに使う道具・材料

織り機… ご紹介している他にも、様々なサイズや形があります。
セロハンテープ… タテ糸を織り機に固定するときに使います。
テグス・ビーズステッチ糸… 糸は作りたいものに合わせて使い分けます。
ビーズ（デリカビーズ）… 織用に開発された最高級のシードビーズは、穴が大きく形が均一で高品質、カラーも豊富です。
糸切りバサミ
織り用針… 専用の長い針で一気にビーズの穴に糸を通します。
ペンチ類… 出来上がった作品に金具を取り付けるときなどに使います。

①手前の糸巻き棒の左側にタテ糸の端をテープで止めて、止め棒に2〜3回巻きつける。スプリングの間に糸を通し、止め棒に糸をかけることを、向こう側→手前側と順に繰り返し、タテ糸を張る。（この時、糸がゆるまないようにしっかり張る）

Tape end of thread on the roller. Wrap one end of thread around one of the clips 2 or 3 times.
Thread the loom while placing one warp in each space of the coils. Wind around the clip at the other side. Repeat this way back and forth (Keep a equal tension on the warps)

②一段目のビーズを通したヨコ糸を、左端のタテ糸に結びつける。

Tie a knot with the left thread over the first warp on the left.

③タテ糸の下からヨコ糸を通し、指でビーズを押し上げるようにして左端から一粒ずつタテ糸の間にビーズを入れる。

Thread the left thread underneath the warp threads. Use your fingers to bring the beads up between the warp threads starting from left to right, with one bead between each pair of warps.

④指でビーズを押し上げながら、針がタテ糸の上を通るようにし、ビーズに通す。

Thread the needle over the warp threads while bringing up the beads with your fingers.

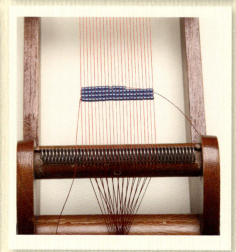

あとがき

　私がビーズ織りに出会ったのは友人と行った八ヶ岳の萌木の村の小さなショップでした。
　ペルーからの輸入品だというそのネックレスの小さく整然と並んだ一粒々々のビーズの煌めきに一目で魅了されてしまったのです。
　何処でこのような作品を作ることが出来るのだろうかと、東京に帰ってすぐに本屋に向かいました。そして探し当てたのがMIYUKIのデリカビーズ織りでした。子育て、学校のPTAの仕事などを終え、何かに挑戦してみようかと思っていた矢先だったので、すぐに教室に通い始めました。
　織りの基本から始まって、色々なテクニックをカリキュラムから学びました。そして、ビーズを織るという繊細な作業を、どのようにして自分の「思い描くもの」へと結び付けていくかと考えながら作品を創り始めました。
　最初の大きい作品が赤い茶箱です。まず思ったのが、地の色は赤にしたい、赤の地に模様が沈まないためには、思い切りあでやかな藤の花や御車…と考えているうちに、絵巻に出てくる源氏物語のイメージが重なって「源氏物語」と題名を付けました。また継ぎ目のない作品を作るにはどうしたらいいのかなど、さまざまな悩みに直面しながら工夫して創り上げました。2009年のBead Dreamsでファイナリストに選ばれた時に苦労は吹き飛んでしまいました。
　二作目の作品が御簾『萌黄色の中に舞う桜』になります。萌黄色と白のビーズで流れをつくり、スワロフスキーをいれて桜の花が舞い散っている様子を表現してみました。タテのビーズとヨコのビーズの色を微妙に変え、軽やかに見せるために織りを工夫して仕上げました。ビーズの数を数えるのにも労力を費やしました。この作品も2010年にファイナリストに選ばれ、困難を乗り越えた甲斐がありました。桜の花はBEAD&BUTTONの生徒にも、とても人気があります。
　作品創りはいつも苦戦の連続でした。しかし、出来上がるとまた新たに湧き上がってくるものがあるのです。また、思いを形にするその一瞬の喜びを求めてこれからも新しい作品を創り上げていきたいと思っております。
　思えば、たくさんの方々にお世話になりました。川本恵美子先生はデパートで拝見したルネッサンスバッグが出会いのきっかけでした。とりどりのビーズの色合いと形、そして西陣の帯地がいまでも目に焼き付いて離れません。優しさあふれるお人柄にすっかりファンになりました。
　川本先生は私の作品を、斉藤正子先生に紹介して下さいました。斉藤先生はイギリスのBeadworkers Guild会員で2013年からGBBSで講師をされていらして、アメリカでの講習も2011年、2012年と活躍されていらっしゃいます。斉藤先生とのご縁で、イギリスのビーズショウで披露する機会を得ました。
　またアメリカのウィスコンシン州ミルウォーキーで行われているBead&Button Showの講師の話は、野末園子先生が背中を押してくださったから実現できたことでした。野末先生は、2005年にBead&Button Showで日本人として初めてオフルームの講師をされ、ずっと今に至っていらっしゃいます。さらにMIYUKIの勝岡常務にはBead&Button Showにエントリーするにあたって、大変お世話になっております。
　最後にビーズ織り「教室」というより「豊田組」ともいえる素晴らしい生徒、切磋琢磨して、作品創りに取り組んでいる皆様に感謝する次第です。翻訳のお手伝いをして下さったヤング美紀子さん、お人形を作って下さっている矢口裕子さん、そしていつも力になってくれている池田茂都枝さんと私の家族にも感謝の念でいっぱいです。有難うございました。

　これからビーズ織りを志す後輩の為に、なにかお役に立てるきっかけになってくれたらとの思いで写真集の出版へと心が動きました。参考にしていただけたら大変幸せです。

2015年 秋　豊田里子

Afterword

The first time I saw a bead weaving work was at a small store at Moegi-Village in the Yatsugatake Mountains during my vacation with a friend. It was a necklace imported from Peru and the brightness of each orderly set bead fascinated me at first sight.

As soon as I returned home to Tokyo, I headed out to a bookstore hoping to find where I could learn to make such works and that is how I found out about Miyuki Delica Beads Weaving.

I started taking classes and it was perfect timing for me because I was just thinking about taking on a new challenge in my life, since my kids were grown up and I had no more PTA work and all.

The class curriculum taught me various techniques and basic weaving. Then I started working on my own pieces, thinking how to connect the delicate bead weaving with "my imagination" and presenting it as a piece of art.

My first big project was a red tea box. First thing I thought was to make the base color red. For the patterns, I did not want them to sink in the base color so I decided to have very vivid wisteria flowers and carriage. While I was thinking about the design, an image of the illustrated handscroll came up and I named my tea box "The Tale of Genji". Making a seamless piece was one of my big challenges and I had to face many other difficulties during the creative process. But all my hard work paid off when my piece was selected as a finalist for the Bead Dreams Contest in 2009.

My second big project was a partition. Fresh yellow-green and white bead created the flow, and I used Swarovski beads to present cherry blossoms falling as if they were dancing. I became more creative with my weaving, changing the color of the beads on the horizontal line slightly from the ones on the vertical line to give an airy impression. Counting the number of beads also needed a great deal of effort. But my struggles were rewarded when this piece was also selected as a finalist for the same contest in 2010. The cherry blossoms were also very popular among my students of the Bead & Button workshops.

Creating a work of beads is always full of challenges and difficulties. However, as soon as I finish a piece, a new idea grows inside me. I would like to continue to create new pieces, pursuing a moment of joy by giving shape to my imagination.

Looking back now, a lot of people have given me their support. I met Ms. Emiko Kawamoto because of her Renaissance style bag at a department store. I still remember the way different shapes and colors of beads were used and the beauty of Nishijin style Obi-materials. Her kind personality made me into one of her fans.

Ms. Kawamoto introduced my works to Ms. Masako Saito, a member of Beadworkers Guild whom had been teaching at the Great British Beads Show (GBBS) since 2013. She helped me to exhibit my work at a beads show in England. She was also a teacher at workshops in the United States in 2011 and 2012.

I was able to take a teaching position at the Bead & Button Show which has been held in Wisconsin, United States every year, because Ms. Sonoko Nozue had given me a supportive push. Ms. Nozue was the first Japanese teacher to teach off-loom beading at the Bead & Button Show in 2005 and continues to teach to this day. Mr. Katsuoka, Executive Director of Miyuki Co., Ltd. has been helping me throughout my time with the Bead & Button Show.

Last but not least; to my great students who are not only just a group of students but more like "Team Toyoda", I really appreciate their dedication for making their works. I am also truly thankful to Mikiko Yang who has helped me with the translations, Yuko Yaguchi who has been making the dolls, Motoe Ikeda and my family who have always supported me in many ways. Thank you all very much.

I decided to publish my book hoping to help those who want to start learning bead weaving. It is my great pleasure if you enjoy my book and find it useful.

豊田里子プロフィール
Profile of Satoko Toyoda

http://beads.ckr.jp

《略歴・経歴》
2000年3月　デリカビーズ織り協会入会
2002年12月　講師認定
2004年6月　準師範認定
2006年6月　師範認定
2003年3月　自宅にて豊田里子ビーズ教室を始める
2003年6月　ユザワヤ芸術学院吉祥寺講師就任
2006年10月　サンケイ・リビングカルチャー倶楽部講師登録
2011年6月　「BEAD&BUTTON SHOW」(USA) 講師
2012年6月　「BEAD&BUTTON SHOW」(USA) 講師
2013年6月　「BEAD&BUTTON SHOW」(USA) 講師
2014年6月　「BEAD&BUTTON SHOW」(USA) 講師
2015年6月　「BEAD&BUTTON SHOW」(USA) 講師
2016年6月　「BEAD&BUTTON SHOW」(USA) 講師予定

《受賞歴》
2008年7月　「ビーズグランプリ2008」佳作　入賞
2009年6月　「BEAD DREAMS 2009」BEST IN SHOW (最優秀賞) Objects or accessories 1st
2010年2月　「世界らん展 日本大賞2010」美術工芸審査部門　特別賞
2010年6月　「BEAD DREAMS 2010」BEST IN SHOW (最優秀賞) Objects or accessories 1st
2011年6月　「BEAD DREAMS 2011」Objects or accessories 3rd
2012年6月　「BEAD DREAMS 2012」Objects or accessories 入賞
2015年6月　「BEAD DREAMS 2015」Objects or accessories 入賞

《展示会》
2005年12月　クリスタルポット(新宿)にて豊田里子デリカビーズ織り展
2008年4月　クリスタルポット(新宿)にて豊田里子ビーズ織り教室作品展
2010年11月　ギャラリーサロンドフルール(南青山)にて豊田里子ビーズ織り教室作品展
2014年11月　ギャラリーサロンドフルール(南青山)にて豊田里子ビーズ織り教室作品展
2015年11月　アクセサリーミュージアム(目黒)にて企画展 Vol.24 予定

<Biography>
March 2000　Became a member of MIYUKI Delica Bead Loom Association
December 2002　Acquired Beading Instructor certification
June 2004　Acquired Associate Beading Master certification
June 2006　Acquired Beading Master certification
March 2003　Started beading class at home
June 2003　Became an instructor at Yuzawaya Art Institute Kichijoji Branch
October 2006　Registered as an instructor at Sankei Living Culture Club
June 2011　Instructor at "Bead & Button Show" (USA)
June 2012　Instructor at "Bead & Button Show" (USA)
June 2013　Instructor at "Bead & Button Show" (USA)
June 2014　Instructor at "Bead & Button Show" (USA)
June 2015　Instructor at "Bead & Button Show" (USA)
June 2016　Instructor at "Bead & Button Show" (USA)-TBD

<Awards>
July 2008　Honorable Mention in Beads Grand-Prix Japan
June 2009　Best-In-Show (highest award) and First Place in Objects or Accessories in BeadDreams 2009
February 2010　Special Award in Arts and Crafts in Japan Grand Prix International Orchid Festival
June 2010　Best-In-Show (highest award) and First Place in Objects or Accessories in BeadDreams 2010
June 2011　3rd Place in Objects or Accessories in BeadDreams 2011
June 2012　Finalist in Objects or Accessories in BeadDreams 2012
June 2015　Finalist in Objects or Accessories in BeadDreams 2015

<Exhibition>
December 2005　Satoko Toyoda Delica Bead Loom Exhibition at Crystal Spot in Shinjuku, Tokyo
April 2008　Satoko Toyoda Delica Bead Loom Class Exhibition at Crystal Spot in Shinjuku, Tokyo
November 2010　Satoko Toyoda Delica Bead Loom Class Exhibition at Gallery Salon de Fleur in Minami-Aoyama, Tokyo
November 2014　Satoko Toyoda Delica Bead Loom Class Exhibition at Gallery Salon de Fleur in Minami-Aoyama, Tokyo
November 2015　Future Exhibition Vol.24 at Accessory Museum in Meguro, Tokyo - TBD

増刊クリエイター no.13

Espoir
煌めくビーズ織りの世界

2015年11月19日　発行

著　者　　豊田里子

翻　訳　　ヤング美紀子
人形制作　矢口裕子
協　力　　アトリエ翔
スペシャルサンクス　池田茂都枝

編　集　　島野聡子
レイアウト　吉川智香子
発行人　　浅井潤一

発行所　　株式会社　亥辰舎
　　　　〒612-8438 京都市伏見区深草フチ町 1-3
　　　　TEL 075-644-8141　FAX 075-644-5225
　　　　http://www.ishinsha.com

印刷所　　土山印刷株式会社

定　価　　本体 1,800円+税
　　　　ISBN978-4-904850-49-7

©SATOKO TOYODA ©ISHINSHA 2015 Printed in Japan
本誌掲載の写真、記事の無断転載を禁じます。